Mom!

What is...?

Volume 2

Complex concepts
made very simple

Dr. Carol Lee

ISBN 978-1-967362-75-2 (paperback)
ISBN 978-1-967362-76-9 (hardcover)
ISBN 978-1-967362-77-6 (digital)

Printed in the United States of America

Contents

Mom, what is honesty?

Mom: Dear, honesty is when you tell the truth, even when you have done something wrong.

Me: But... you may get mad.

Mom: Not as mad as if you don't tell the truth and then I find out the truth later.

Me: Right.

Mom: And if you don't tell the truth, people will not believe what you say next time, and they will lose respect in you.

Me: Mom, what is respect?

Mom, what is respect?

Mom: Respect is when someone thinks that you are good at what you do, and believes in you. They may even look up to you.

Me: Like how I look up to my piano teacher because she is so good at playing the piano?

Mom: Yes! Respect does not just come from being good at something, but also comes from the fact that she is nice and treats other people nicely.

Me: I see. I don't want to ever change piano teachers!

Mom: That means she has gained your loyalty as well.

Me: Mom, what is loyalty?

Mom, what is loyalty?

Mom: Loyalty is remaining true to and believing in something and not ever wanting to leave it. It can be a person, a public figure or team, or an object.

Me: Oh, like you never wanting to leave me?

Mom: Yes, I will be loyal to you. And when daddy and I got married, we made vows to be loyal to each other.

Me: My friend's parents are leaving each other in a divorce. Mom, what is a divorce?

Mom, what is divorce?

Mom: A divorce is when two people decide that they no longer want to be together.

Me: But why?

Mom: Well, there can be many reasons, and every case is different.

Me: Hmmm...but that is so sad.

Mom: It is a personal choice, and like I said, there are many reasons that lead to divorce. I am sure everyone tries their best before they come to that decision.

Me: I hope that you and daddy will not divorce.

Mom: I think one thing that holds two people together for a long time is appreciation of each other.

Me: Mom, what is appreciation?

Mom, what is appreciation?

Mom: Appreciation is when you like what people do, and what makes them who they are. For example, I appreciate that you made your bed yesterday.

Me: And I appreciate that you cook for me!

Mom: Thank you! Remember, you will always find nice things in others that you can appreciate. Even in times of anger. You would like others to appreciate and like what you are and what you do too, right?

Me: Yes. It makes me happy to be liked!

Mom: Yes, and it should make you happy to like others too. With appreciation comes humility.

Me: Mom, what is humility?

Mom, what is humility?

Mom: Humility is when you serve others, put others before you, and always think about others first, instead of being proud about yourself or what you can do.

Me: But even when I am good at something?

Mom: Yes. You can be good at something, but always remember that there will be other people who are better than you. And in order to be better, you have to know that you are not the best and there is room to do better.

Me: Oh I see.

Mom: With humility comes curiosity because you know that there is always more to learn.

Me: Mom, what is curiosity?

13

Mom, what is curiosity?

Mom: Curiosity is when you want to find out about something. So it helps you learn about new things.

Me: Like how I want to learn about how the human body works?

Mom: Yes. Curiosity pushes you to find new information about things. Why don't you go and write a list of things you want to learn about?

The
END

Things to learn: